What's for lunch?

Chocolate

Claire Llewellyn

W

FRANKLIN WATTS
LONDON • SYDNEY

What's for lunch?

Chocolate

This edition 2003

Franklin Watts
96 Leonard Street
London
EC2A 4XD

Franklin Watts Australia
45-51 Huntley Street
Alexandria
NSW 2015

Editor: Samantha Armstrong
Series Designer: Kirstie Billingham
Designer: Kelly Flynn
Consultant: Cadbury Ltd
Reading Consultant: Prue Goodwin, Reading and Language
Information Centre, Reading

A CIP catalogue record for this book is available from the British Library
Dewey Decimal Classification Number 641.3

ISBN: 0 7496 4943 7

Printed in Hong Kong, China

Today we are having chocolate cake.
It is a special treat.
It contains **sugar** and **fat**,
and gives us **energy**.

Chocolate is made from **cocoa beans**
which grow on cocoa trees.
The trees grow in warm,
wet parts of the world,
on large farms called **plantations**.

6

Tiny flowers grow on the trees.
After a few weeks,
the flowers develop into **pods**.
Cocoa beans grow inside the pods.
There are thirty or forty beans
inside each pod.

Farmers take great care
of the **crop**.
They spray the trees
with **insecticide**
to protect them from
pests and **diseases**.
Sometimes they give
them extra water.

After about six months,
when the pods have turned
a reddish-orange colour,
the farmers use knives to cut them down.
They split the pods open
and remove the cocoa beans.

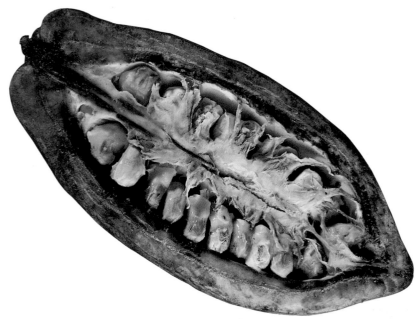

The beans are spread out
to dry in the sun for a week
and turned regularly.
This makes sure they
don't go **mouldy**.
Then the dried beans
are put into sacks
and taken to factories.

14

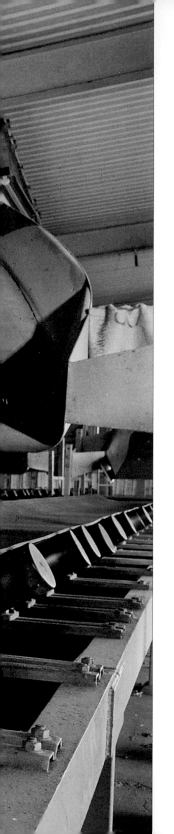

At the factories
the sacks of beans are cut open
and any insects or bits of cocoa plant
are picked out.

The beans are cleaned and **roasted**
to bring out their flavour.
Then the beans are **ground** until they
become a runny, fatty cream,
called **cocoa mass**.

Sometimes all the liquid
is squeezed out of the cocoa mass
until it leaves a solid block of cocoa
that can be ground into powder.
Cocoa powder is used
to make chocolate drinks.
Or it can add a chocolate flavour
to sauces, cakes and ice-cream.

To make chocolate for sweets,
the cocoa mass is mixed with milk and sugar.
Specially-trained **tasters** check the chocolate
to make sure that it looks, tastes
and feels just right.

The chocolate is poured into **moulds**, and chilled until it is hard. Sometimes, nuts, **raisins** or puffed rice are mixed in with the chocolate.

Bars of chocolate are wrapped in **foil**
to keep them fresh.
Then they are delivered to shops
ready for people to buy.

Chocolate can be made into
all sorts of different shapes.

Most people love chocolate.
It is sweet and delicious and
always a special treat.

Glossary

cocoa beans	the seeds of the cocoa tree
cocoa mass	the cream that comes from ground cocoa beans
cocoa powder	ground cocoa beans used for flavouring
crop	what farmers grow in their fields
disease	something that attacks plants or animals
energy	the strength to work and play
fat	something found in food that gives us energy
foil	metal that is made into thin sheets and used to wrap food to keep it fresh
ground	crushed into small bits
insecticide	something that kills insects
mould	a tray with a special shape. When chocolate sets it takes on the shape of the mould

mouldy	to be covered with growth and bad to eat
pest	an animal such as a beetle or fly that spoils or destroys crops
plantation	a large piece of land used to grow just one type of plant like cocoa trees
pod	the part of a plant that grows on the cocoa tree and contains the cocoa beans
raisin	a sweet grape that has been dried
roasted	cooked in an oven
sugar	something that is added to food or drink to make them taste sweet
tasters	people who eat small amounts of chocolate to make sure it tastes just right

Index

Picture credits: Cadbury Ltd. 12. 16-17, 19, 26; Holt Studios International: 6-7, 8, 9, 10, 11, 14 (all Nigel Cattlin); Panos Pictures (Crispin Hughes) 14-15; Robert Harding 13; Rowntree-Nestle Ltd. 24; Zefa-Bramaz 23; Steve Shott cover; All other photographs Tim Ridley, Wells Street Studios, London.
With thanks to Scarlett Carney and Thomas Ong.